SECRETS TO OVERCOME ADVERSITY

STRATEGIES FOR COPING WITH DIFFICULT TIMES

DR. JAGADEESH PILLAI

Made with ♥ on the Notion Press Platform
www.notionpress.com

|| Dedicated to all wisdom seekers around the World ||

৺

Contents

Contents

Prayer

**"Om Bhadram Karnebhih Shrunuyaama
DevaahBhadram Pashyemaakshabhiryajatraah
SthirairangaistushtuvaamsastanoobhihVyashema
Devahitam YadaayuhSwasti Na Indro
VridhashravaahSwasti Nah Pooshaa
VishwavedaahSwasti Nastaarkshyo ArishtanemihSwasti
No Brihaspatir DadhaatuOm Shantih, Shantih, Shantih"**

The literal meaning of this mantra is: OM. O Gods! Let us
hear auspicious words from our ears. O reverent Gods! Let
us behold propitious visions from our eyes, let our organs
and body be stable, healthy, and strong. Let us do that
which is pleasing to the gods in the life span allotted to us.
May Indra, inscribed in the scriptures, bring us fortune!
May Pushan, the knower of the world, grant us prosperity!
May Trakshya, who vanquishes enemies, bestow us with
blessings! May Brihaspati bring us success!
OM Peace, Peace, Peace.

৪৩

ABOUT THE AUTHOR

Dr. Jagadeesh Pillai is a renowned Guinness World Record holder, writer, and researcher hailing from Varanasi, also known as the abode of Lord Shiva. With a Ph.D. in Vedic Science and a range of creative ideas and achievements, he is a true polymath. He is the author of more than 100 books including Research Publications. Although his roots can be traced back to Kerala, the people of Varanasi hold him in high regard and affectionately consider him one of their own.

In 1998, Dr. Pillai was offered a job at Banaras Hindu University, but he left the position after only two months to pursue greater goals in life. He believed that in order to study Indian scriptures and engage in other creative endeavours, he needed to retire from the daily grind of working solely for money at a young age.

He started an export business from scratch, using the knowledge he had gained from a previous job in the industry. His intelligence and unique approach to business led to great success in a short period of time, earning him more in just a decade and a half than he would have in a lifetime working in a government job. Upon the passing of Dr. APJ Abdul Kalam, Dr. Pillai decided to leave the business and dedicate himself to reading, studying, researching, and experimenting.

During his tenure in the export business, Dr. Pillai traveled to over 16 countries, gaining valuable insight and experiencing the world and life in detail.

Dr. Pillai has achieved four Guinness World Records in the following subjects:

"Script to Screen" - In this record, Dr. Pillai produced and directed an animation film within the shortest time possible, breaking the previous record set by Canadians. He has also received numerous national and international awards and recognitions for this achievement.

Longest Line of Postcards - For this record, Dr. Pillai created a line of 16,300 postcards on the occasion of the 163rd anniversary of Indian Postal Day. The event also included a questionnaire about the Indian flag.

Largest Poster Awareness Campaign - Dr. Pillai designed an awareness campaign on the subject of "Beti Bachao - Beti Padhao" (Save the Girl Child - Educate the Girl Child) to achieve this record.

Largest Envelope - In tribute to the Indian Prime Minister's "Make in India" initiative, Dr. Pillai created a 4000 square meter envelope using waste paper to achieve this record.

Attempted - **70000 Candles on a 210 kg Cake** - To celebrate the 70th Indian Independence Day, Dr. Pillai attempted to light 70,000 candles on a 210 kg cake, which was recorded in World Records India.

Attempted - **Documentary on Dhamek Stupa of Sarnath in 17 Languages** - Dr. Pillai attempted to create a documentary on the Dhamek Stupa of Sarnath, dubbing it in 17 different languages. The result of this attempt is currently awaiting confirmation from the Guinness World Records.

Dr. Pillai is skilled in teaching the Bhagavad Gita, a Hindu scripture, and is popular among young people. He has helped many young people improve their lives through his motivational teachings.

In addition to teaching, he has composed and sung numerous Sanskrit Bhajans and patriotic songs.

He has also written and directed several short films and documentaries for awareness campaigns, and has volunteered with the police in both UP and Kerala to spread awareness about various issues through videos and photography.

Incredibly, he has produced and directed over 100 documentaries about the city of Varanasi, all on his own.

He has also helped and guided more than 25 boys and girls to achieve world records through creative and innovative methods. He is a multifaceted person who uses his intellect and the blessings given to him by God to excel in various areas. He is both a teacher and a student, always learning and teaching, and is able to master any subject he comes across.

He is a selfless social activist and motivational speaker who has overcome struggles and failures to become a successful and enthusiastic individual with a rich life experience.

In addition to his work with the Bhagavad Gita, he is also an efficient Tarot card reader, Astro-Vastu consultant, and a talented singer and composer. He has sung the entire Ram Charita Manas and Bhagavad Gita in his own compositions, and has sung the phrase "Lokah Samastha Sukhino Bhavantu" in 50 different languages. He is currently working on a detailed and scientific study of Vedas, Upanishads, Puranas, and the Bhagavad Gita. He has also composed and sung the Hanuman Chalisa and Gayatri Mantra in 108 and 1008 different compositions, respectively.

Awards - Four Times Guinness World Records, Winner of Mahatma Gandhi Vishwa Shanti Puraskar, Mahatma Gandhi Global Peace Ambassador, Kashi Ratna Award, Dr. APJ Abdul Kalam Motivational Person of the Year 2017, Mother Teresa Award, Indira Gandhi Priyadarshini Award, Bharat Vikas Ratna Award, Udyog Ratna Award, Vigyan Prasar Award, Poorvanchal Ratn Samman.

Preface

Adversity is a part of life, and it can be difficult to navigate the challenges and hardships that come our way. However, it is important to remember that adversity can also be a source of growth and learning. By embracing the right strategies and developing the right mindset, individuals can overcome adversity and find resilience in the face of difficulties.

In this book, "Secrets to Overcome Adversity: Strategies for Coping with Difficult Times," we explore the many ways that individuals can overcome adversity and find strength in the face of challenges. From mindfulness and self-compassion to positive thinking and building support systems, this book provides a comprehensive guide to coping with difficult times.

Whether you are facing a personal challenge or simply looking to build resilience and strength, this book will provide you with the tools you need to overcome adversity and find success in life.

I

Understanding Adversity and Its Impact on Coping

Adversity is an inevitable part of life. It is defined as a difficult or unpleasant situation that presents challenges and obstacles, such as a physical illness, financial problems, relationship issues, or the loss of a loved one. Adversity can be overwhelming and can impact a person's well-being, both physically and emotionally. However, adversity can also be a catalyst for growth and personal development. In this chapter, we will explore the concept of adversity and its impact on coping.

Adversity can come in many forms, such as natural disasters, personal tragedy, or workplace stress. It can be a one-time event or a series of events that can cause a long-term impact. Adversity can challenge a person's beliefs, values, and perceptions, leading to feelings of fear, uncertainty, and sadness. It can also lead to physical symptoms, such as headaches, fatigue, and sleep disturbances.

The impact of adversity on coping varies from person to person, and it depends on several factors, such as a person's coping skills, resilience, and support system. People who have strong coping skills and support systems are more likely to bounce back from adversity and recover more quickly. On the other hand, those who lack coping skills and support systems are more likely to experience long-term consequences, such as depression, anxiety, and chronic stress.

Adversity can also have a lasting impact on a person's life, changing the way they see the world and the way they approach life's challenges. However, it is important to remember that adversity is not a life sentence, and it is possible to overcome its effects. By developing coping strategies and seeking support, people can find hope and resilience in the face of adversity.

Adversity is an inevitable part of life, and it can have a significant impact on coping. Understanding the nature of adversity and its impact on coping is the first step in learning how to overcome adversity and find hope and resilience in the face of difficult times. In the following chapters of this book, we will explore various strategies and techniques that can help people overcome adversity and find the strength to cope with difficult times.

※

"Adversity is not something to be overcome,
but a challenge to be embraced."

∞

II

Recognizing and Managing Negative Emotions

Adversity can bring a range of negative emotions, such as fear, anger, sadness, and anxiety. It is important to recognize and understand these emotions, as they can have a significant impact on mental and physical well-being. In this chapter, we will explore ways to recognize and manage negative emotions, and how to use them as tools for growth and personal development.

The first step in managing negative emotions is to recognize them. This can be done by paying attention to physical sensations, such as a tight chest, shallow breathing, or a racing heartbeat, as well as to thoughts and feelings, such as anger, sadness, or anxiety. Once negative emotions are recognized, it is important to acknowledge and validate them. This means accepting that the emotions are there, and giving yourself permission to feel them.

The next step is to manage negative emotions, and this can be done in several ways, such as practicing relaxation techniques, mindfulness, and cognitive-behavioral therapy. Relaxation techniques, such as deep breathing, meditation, and yoga, can help reduce stress and anxiety and promote relaxation. Mindfulness is the practice of being present and fully engaged in the moment, and it can help reduce negative thoughts and emotions. Cognitive-behavioral therapy is a form of therapy that focuses on changing negative thought patterns, and it can be a powerful tool for managing negative emotions.

In addition to these techniques, it is also important to seek support from friends, family, or a mental health professional. Support from others can provide comfort and encouragement, and it can help reduce the impact of negative emotions. Furthermore, it is important to engage in activities that bring joy and meaning, such as exercise, hobbies, or volunteering, as these activities can provide a sense of purpose and fulfillment, and help boost overall well-being.

Recognizing and managing negative emotions is an important part of coping with adversity. By using techniques, such as relaxation, mindfulness, therapy, and seeking support, people can learn to manage negative emotions, and use them as tools for growth and personal development. In the next chapter, we will explore the importance of self-care and how it can help overcome adversity and promote well-being.

&

DR. JAGADEESH PILLAI

"Challenges are what make life interesting
and overcoming them is what makes life
meaningful."

III

Setting Realistic Goals and Prioritizing Self-Care

Adversity can leave people feeling overwhelmed and drained, making it difficult to set and achieve goals. In this chapter, we will explore the importance of setting realistic goals and prioritizing self-care, and how they can help overcome adversity and promote well-being.

Setting realistic goals is a key part of coping with adversity.

Goals provide a sense of direction and purpose, and they help people focus on what is important. However, it is important to set realistic goals that are achievable, and that align with personal values and priorities. It is also important to break goals down into smaller, achievable steps, and to celebrate progress along the way.

Self-care is another important part of coping with adversity.

Self-care refers to activities and practices that promote physical, emotional, and mental well-being. Examples of self-care include exercise, healthy eating, sleep, and relaxation. Self-care is essential for overcoming adversity, as it provides the energy and resources needed to face life's challenges.

In addition to exercise and relaxation, it is important to ***prioritize self-care by setting aside time*** for activities that bring joy and meaning. This can include hobbies, volunteering, or spending time with loved ones. It is also important to engage in activities that promote a positive outlook, such as gratitude and positive self-talk. These activities can help reduce the impact of negative emotions, and promote resilience and well-being.

Finally, it is important to ***seek help and support from others when needed.*** This can include seeking support from friends, family, or a mental health professional. Support from others can provide comfort, encouragement, and practical help, and it can also help reduce the impact of negative emotions.

Setting realistic goals and prioritizing self-care are important parts of coping with adversity. By setting goals, engaging in self-care activities, and seeking support from others, people can find hope, resilience, and well-being in the face of adversity. In the next chapter, we will explore the importance of resilience and how it can help overcome adversity and promote well-being.

"Success is not final, failure is not fatal: it is the courage to continue that counts."

୫

IV

Building Resilience and Coping with Setbacks

Adversity can bring setbacks and challenges, and it is important to have the resilience and coping skills to handle them. In this chapter, we will explore the importance of building resilience and coping with setbacks, and how they can help overcome adversity and promote well-being.

Resilience refers to the ability to bounce back from adversity and to continue moving forward, despite challenges. Building resilience is an important part of coping with adversity, as it provides the strength and flexibility needed to face life's challenges. There are several ways to build resilience, including:

Developing a positive outlook:

Having a positive outlook can help reduce the impact of negative emotions and promote resilience. This can be done by focusing on strengths, practicing gratitude, and engaging in positive self-talk.

Building a support network:

Having a supportive network of friends, family, or a mental health professional can provide comfort, encouragement, and practical help in times of need.

Practicing stress-management techniques:

Engaging in stress-management techniques, such as deep breathing, mindfulness, and exercise, can help reduce stress and promote resilience.

Building coping skills:

Coping skills are strategies that can be used to manage difficult emotions, thoughts, and situations. Examples of coping skills include problem-solving, communication, and mindfulness.

In addition to building resilience, it is also important to cope with setbacks and challenges that may arise. Coping with setbacks can be done in several ways, including:

Acknowledging and validating emotions:

It is important to acknowledge and validate feelings of disappointment, frustration, or sadness, and to give yourself permission to feel them.

Seeking support:

Seeking support from friends, family, or a mental health professional can provide comfort, encouragement, and practical help.

Reframing setbacks as opportunities for growth:

Setbacks can be seen as opportunities for growth, learning, and personal development. Reframing setbacks in this way can help reduce their impact and promote resilience.

Taking action:

Taking action, such as setting new goals, engaging in self-care activities, or seeking help, can help overcome setbacks and move forward.

Building resilience and coping with setbacks are important parts of coping with adversity. By building resilience, engaging in self-care activities, seeking support, and taking action, people can find hope, resilience, and well-being in the face of adversity. In the next chapter, we will explore the importance of hope and how it can help overcome adversity and promote well-being.

"Adversity builds character and strengthens
the spirit."

∞

V

Overcoming Procrastination and Perfectionism

Procrastination and perfectionism are common obstacles that can interfere with our ability to overcome adversity and cope with difficult times. In this chapter, we will explore the impact of procrastination and perfectionism, and strategies for overcoming them.

Procrastination is the tendency to delay tasks or put them off until later. It can be a major obstacle to success, as it can prevent us from taking action and making progress towards our goals. Some common reasons for procrastination include fear of failure, lack of motivation, and feeling overwhelmed.

To overcome procrastination, it is important to:

Set clear and achievable goals:

Having clear and achievable goals can provide motivation and direction, and reduce the tendency to procrastinate.

Break down tasks into smaller steps:

Breaking down large tasks into smaller, manageable steps can make them less overwhelming and easier to start.

Use positive self-talk:

Encouraging yourself with positive self-talk can help reduce the impact of negative thoughts and increase motivation.

Eliminate distractions:

Identifying and eliminating distractions can help increase focus and productivity, and reduce the tendency to procrastinate.

Perfectionism is the tendency to hold oneself to extremely high standards, and to feel overly critical of one's own performance. It can be a major obstacle to success, as it can prevent us from taking action and making progress towards our goals. Some common reasons for perfectionism include fear of failure, low self-esteem, and a need for control.

To overcome perfectionism, it is important to:

Set realistic and achievable goals:

Setting realistic and achievable goals can reduce the pressure to be perfect, and increase the likelihood of success.

Practice self-compassion:

Practicing self-compassion, such as forgiving yourself for mistakes, and accepting yourself for who you are, can help reduce the impact of perfectionism.

Focus on the process, not just the outcome:

Focusing on the process, such as learning and growing, rather than just the outcome, can help reduce the pressure to be perfect.

Celebrate progress and successes:

Celebrating progress and successes, no matter how small, can help increase self-esteem and reduce the impact of perfectionism.

In conclusion, procrastination and perfectionism are common obstacles that can interfere with our ability to overcome adversity and cope with difficult times. By setting clear and achievable goals, breaking down tasks into smaller steps, practicing self-compassion, and celebrating progress and successes, people can overcome these obstacles and promote well-being. In the next chapter, we will explore the importance of self-compassion and how it can help overcome adversity and promote well-being.

"It's not how we handle success, but how we
handle adversity that defines our character."

ꙮ

VI

Understanding the Power of Positive Thinking and Gratitude

Positive thinking and gratitude are powerful tools that can help people overcome adversity and cope with difficult times. In this chapter, we will explore the impact of positive thinking and gratitude, and strategies for promoting them. Positive thinking is the act of focusing on the positive aspects of life, and looking for opportunities in challenges. It can help people to overcome adversity by reducing stress and anxiety, increasing motivation and resilience, and improving overall well-being. To promote positive thinking, it is important to:

Practice gratitude: Gratitude involves taking time to acknowledge and appreciate the good things in life, and can help shift focus towards the positive.

Surround yourself with positive people: Surrounding yourself with positive, optimistic individuals can have a significant impact on your outlook on life and help you maintain a positive perspective.

Keep a gratitude journal: Writing down what you are thankful for each day can help cultivate a sense of gratitude and positivity.

Engage in positive self-talk: Reframe negative thoughts into positive ones, and practice talking to yourself in a supportive and encouraging manner.

Engage in physical activity: Regular exercise can help improve mood, reduce stress, and increase overall well-being.

Focus on solutions: Instead of dwelling on problems, focus on finding solutions and taking action towards resolving them.

Express gratitude to others: Saying thank you to others, and expressing appreciation for their actions, can foster feelings of gratitude.

Practice mindfulness: Taking the time to focus on the present moment and appreciate it can increase feelings of gratitude.

By incorporating positive thinking and gratitude into daily

life, individuals can improve their well-being and cope with life's challenges more effectively.

Lastly, it's important to remember that promoting positive thinking and gratitude takes effort and practice, but the benefits can have a profound impact on your life.

"The greatest glory in living lies not in never falling, but in rising every time we fall."

VII

Building Support Systems and Connecting with Others

One of the most important strategies for overcoming adversity is building a strong support system and connecting with others. Having a network of supportive individuals can provide emotional and practical assistance, boost one's resilience, and help them to cope with difficult times. This chapter will explore the benefits of building support systems and connecting with others, and strategies for doing so.

Why Building Support Systems is Important

Having a strong support system can provide individuals with a sense of security and comfort during difficult times.

It can help to reduce stress and anxiety, increase self-esteem, and improve overall well-being. In addition, having a supportive network can provide practical assistance, such as help with tasks, advice, and resources. Furthermore, connecting with others can help to increase feelings of belonging, and foster a sense of community and connection.

Strategies for Building Support Systems

Identify people you can trust:

Start by identifying individuals in your life that you trust and feel comfortable turning to for support. This could include friends, family members, co-workers, or mental health professionals.

Cultivate relationships:

Building strong relationships takes time and effort. Reach out to others, share your thoughts and feelings, and spend time doing things together. This can help to deepen your connections and create a supportive network.

Join a support group:

Joining a support group can provide an opportunity to connect with others who are facing similar challenges. Support groups can offer a sense of community and provide a platform for sharing experiences and offering advice.

Seek professional help:

Mental health professionals, such as therapists and counselors, can provide support and guidance during difficult times. Seeking help from a professional can help to improve mental health and well-being, and provide coping strategies for dealing with adversity.

Volunteer or engage in community activities:

Volunteering or participating in community activities can help to build relationships and provide a sense of purpose. It can also increase feelings of fulfillment and satisfaction, and improve overall well-being.

Building a strong support system and connecting with others can play a vital role in overcoming adversity and coping with difficult times. By utilizing these strategies, individuals can foster a sense of community, increase resilience, and improve their overall well-being.

"Adversity is the foundation of growth and
the birthplace of strength."

ଛ

VIII

Finding Purpose and Meaning in Difficult Times

Finding purpose and meaning can play a significant role in overcoming adversity and coping with difficult times. When individuals feel that their life has a sense of direction and purpose, it can provide a sense of motivation and hope, even in the face of adversity. This chapter will explore the importance of finding purpose and meaning, and strategies for doing so.

Why Finding Purpose and Meaning is Important

Having a sense of purpose and meaning can provide individuals with a sense of direction and motivation, even in the face of adversity. It can increase resilience, reduce stress and anxiety, and improve overall well-being. In addition, having a clear sense of purpose can help individuals to prioritize their time and energy, and make more meaningful contributions to their communities.

Strategies for Finding Purpose and Meaning

Reflect on your values:

Take time to reflect on what is important to you, and what you value most in life. Consider what makes you feel fulfilled and what you want to achieve in life.

Set goals:

Setting goals can provide a sense of direction and purpose. Make sure to set achievable goals that align with your values and what you want to accomplish in life.

Engage in activities that bring fulfillment:

Engage in activities that bring you joy and fulfillment. This could include hobbies, volunteering, or pursuing personal interests.

Help others:

Making a difference in someone else's life can bring a sense of purpose and fulfillment. Consider volunteering, helping a friend or neighbor, or participating in community service activities.

Cultivate a growth mindset:

Embracing a growth mindset and focusing on personal

development can help to find purpose and meaning. Look for opportunities to learn new skills, try new experiences, and grow as a person.

Finding purpose and meaning can play a significant role in overcoming adversity and improving overall well-being. By utilizing these strategies, individuals can find direction, motivation, and hope, even in the face of challenges.

"The best way to overcome adversity is to embrace it and use it as an opportunity to grow."

೮೨

IX
Managing Stress and Anxiety

Stress and anxiety can be a natural response to adversity, and can have a negative impact on physical and mental health. In this chapter, we will explore the impact of stress and anxiety, and strategies for managing these emotions in difficult times.

Understanding Stress and Anxiety

Stress is a normal response to perceived threats, and can be a natural part of life. It can be triggered by events such as work, relationships, health problems, or financial difficulties. Anxiety, on the other hand, is a feeling of unease, such as worry or fear, that can be out of proportion to the situation. Chronic stress and anxiety can have a negative impact on physical and mental health, and can interfere with daily activities.

Strategies for Managing Stress and Anxiety

Practice relaxation techniques:

Relaxation techniques, such as deep breathing, meditation, and yoga, can help to reduce stress and anxiety. Regular practice can improve physical and mental well-being.

Exercise regularly:

Regular physical activity can help to manage stress and anxiety, and improve overall well-being. Exercise can also improve sleep, boost mood, and reduce feelings of anxiety and depression.

Maintain a healthy diet:

Eating a healthy and balanced diet can help to manage stress and anxiety. Avoiding caffeine and sugar can also help to reduce feelings of stress and anxiety.

Get adequate sleep:

Getting adequate sleep is important for managing stress and anxiety. Aim for 7-9 hours of sleep per night, and establish a consistent sleep routine.

Connect with others:

Connecting with others and building a support network can help to manage stress and anxiety. Spending time with friends, family, or participating in activities with others can improve overall well-being.

Managing stress and anxiety is an important part of overcoming adversity and improving overall well-being. By utilizing these strategies, individuals can reduce feelings of stress and anxiety, and improve their physical and mental health.

"The greatest glory in life is not never falling,
but rising every time we fall."

ઉ

X

The Role of Mindfulness and Self-Compassion

Mindfulness and self-compassion are important tools that can help individuals to overcome adversity and improve overall well-being. In this chapter, we will explore the impact of mindfulness and self-compassion, and strategies for promoting these qualities.

The Importance of Mindfulness

Mindfulness is the practice of paying attention to the present moment, without judgment. It involves focusing on one's thoughts, feelings, and sensations, and accepting them as they are. Mindfulness can help individuals to manage stress and anxiety, improve their mood, and enhance overall well-being.

The Benefits of Self-Compassion

Self-compassion involves being kind and understanding to oneself, especially during difficult times. It involves recognizing that everyone experiences hardship, and treating oneself with the same compassion and care that one would offer to a friend. Self-compassion can improve mood, reduce stress and anxiety, and enhance overall well-being.

Strategies for Promoting Mindfulness and Self-Compassion

Practice mindfulness meditation: Mindfulness meditation is a form of mindfulness that involves focusing on the present moment. Regular practice can improve mental and physical health, and reduce feelings of stress and anxiety.

Engage in self-reflection: Take time to reflect on your thoughts and feelings, and to practice self-compassion. Try to be kind and understanding to yourself, and recognize that everyone experiences hardship.

Practice gratitude: Take time to acknowledge and appreciate the good things in life. This can help to shift focus towards the positive, and improve overall well-being.

Seek support: Connect with others and seek support when needed. Talking to friends, family, or a therapist can help to manage stress and anxiety, and improve overall well-being.

Mindfulness and self-compassion are important tools for overcoming adversity and improving overall well-being. By utilizing these strategies, individuals can manage stress and anxiety, improve their mood, and enhance their physical and mental health.

"The darkest hour is just before the dawn.
Find hope in the darkest of times."

༺༻

XI

Dealing with Failure and Learning from Mistakes

Failure is an inevitable part of life, but it can also be an opportunity for growth and learning. In this chapter, we will explore the impact of failure, and strategies for coping with it and learning from mistakes.

The Impact of Failure

Failure can be a difficult and challenging experience. It can lead to feelings of disappointment, frustration, and shame. However, it is important to recognize that failure is a natural and inevitable part of life, and can provide valuable opportunities for growth and learning.

Strategies for Coping with Failure

Acknowledge your feelings: It is important to recognize and acknowledge the emotions that come with failure. Allow yourself to feel disappointed, frustrated, or sad, and give yourself time to process these emotions.

Reframe the situation: Try to see failure as an opportunity for growth and learning, rather than a personal failure. Ask yourself what you can learn from the situation, and how you can apply this learning to future challenges.

Seek support: Connect with friends, family, or a therapist to discuss your feelings and to get support during difficult times.

Strategies for Learning from Mistakes

Reflect on the situation: Take time to reflect on the situation and identify what went wrong. Ask yourself what you could have done differently, and what you can learn from the experience.

Focus on solutions: Instead of dwelling on the problem, focus on finding solutions and taking action to improve the situation.

Apply your learning: Use the lessons you have learned to improve your performance in the future.

Dealing with failure and learning from mistakes is an important part of overcoming adversity and improving overall well-being. By utilizing these strategies, individuals can transform failure into an opportunity for growth and learning, and use these experiences to build resilience and overcome future challenges.

"Adversity has the power to make us stronger,
if we let it."

&

XII

Understanding and Managing Trauma

Trauma is a profound and often debilitating experience that can have lasting effects on individuals and communities. In this chapter, we will explore the nature of trauma, its impact on individuals and communities, and strategies for coping and recovery.

The Nature of Trauma

Trauma can take many forms, including physical, emotional, or psychological abuse, neglect, or exposure to violence, natural disasters, or other traumatic events. The impact of trauma can be profound and long-lasting, affecting individuals and communities in a variety of ways.

The Impact of Trauma

The impact of trauma can be far-reaching and profound,

affecting individuals and communities in a variety of ways. Some common effects of trauma include anxiety, depression, post-traumatic stress disorder (PTSD), difficulty forming relationships, and physical health problems.

Strategies for Coping with Trauma

Seek professional help: If you are experiencing symptoms of trauma, it is important to seek professional help. A therapist or counselor can help you process your feelings and develop strategies for coping and recovery.

Connect with others: Support from friends, family, or a support group can be invaluable in helping individuals cope with trauma.

Practice self-care: Engaging in activities that promote physical, emotional, and spiritual well-being can help individuals manage the effects of trauma. This may include exercise, meditation, or engaging in a creative activity.

Seek support from community resources: Community resources, such as hotlines or support groups, can provide valuable support for individuals who have experienced trauma.

Reframe the experience: Reframing the traumatic experience in a positive light can help individuals find meaning and purpose in their suffering and develop a sense of resilience.

Managing trauma is a complex and often long-term process, but with the right support and resources, individuals can overcome its effects and build resilience for the future. By understanding the nature of trauma and utilizing these strategies, individuals can take an important step towards healing and recovery.

"The challenges we face today will determine the strength we will have for tomorrow."

॰

XIII

Building Inner Strength through Adversity

Adversity can be a powerful tool for building inner strength and resilience. In this chapter, we will explore how individuals can harness the power of adversity to develop greater inner strength and resilience, and how to apply these skills to future challenges.

The Power of Adversity

Adversity has the power to test our limits and push us to our limits. It can also help us build inner strength by forcing us to confront our fears, develop new coping skills, and build resilience. By facing and overcoming adversity, we can become more confident, self-assured, and capable of handling future challenges.

Strategies for Building Inner Strength through Adversity

Embrace challenges: Rather than avoiding challenges, embrace them as opportunities to build inner strength and resilience. By confronting challenges head-on, individuals can develop a sense of control and mastery over their circumstances.

Develop a growth mindset: Adopt a growth mindset by viewing challenges as opportunities for growth and learning, rather than as insurmountable obstacles.

Cultivate resilience: Develop resilience by engaging in activities that promote mental toughness, such as exercise, mindfulness, or seeking support from others.

Practice self-compassion: Be kind and gentle with yourself as you work through challenges. Self-compassion can help individuals maintain a positive outlook and find meaning in difficult experiences.

Seek support: Surround yourself with supportive individuals who will encourage and uplift you during difficult times.

Building inner strength through adversity requires intentional effort and perseverance, but the benefits are substantial. By developing inner strength, individuals can build resilience and become better equipped to handle future challenges, both in their personal and professional lives.

౭౦

"Overcoming adversity is not about avoiding challenges, it's about facing them with courage and resilience."

XIV

Finding Hope in the Darkest of Times

Hope is a powerful motivator and a source of comfort in difficult times. In this chapter, we will explore how individuals can find hope even in the darkest of times, and how to use it as a tool for overcoming adversity.

The Power of Hope

Hope is a vital component of resilience and can help individuals persevere in the face of adversity. By focusing on positive possibilities and a brighter future, hope can provide a sense of comfort and motivation, even in the most challenging of circumstances.

Strategies for Finding Hope in Difficult Times

Reframe challenges: Reframe challenges as opportunities for growth and learning. This shift in perspective can help individuals find meaning in difficult experiences and maintain a sense of hope.

Cultivate a positive outlook: Focus on the positive aspects of life, and look for opportunities in challenges. Cultivating a positive outlook can help individuals find hope in difficult times.

Surround yourself with supportive individuals: Surrounding yourself with individuals who offer encouragement, support, and positivity can help maintain hope in difficult times.

Engage in meaningful activities: Engaging in meaningful activities, such as volunteering, pursuing hobbies, or spending time with loved ones, can provide a sense of purpose and help maintain hope.

Seek professional support: If necessary, seek professional support, such as therapy or counseling, to help maintain hope and overcome adversity.

Finding hope in difficult times can be challenging, but it is essential for overcoming adversity. By focusing on positive possibilities and engaging in meaningful activities, individuals can maintain hope and persevere in the face of adversity.

"Adversity is not a hindrance, but a path to
growth and learning."

❧

XV

Conclusion: Putting it All Together and Coping with Adversity

In this final chapter, we will bring together all of the strategies and secrets discussed in this book and explore how individuals can use them to overcome adversity and cope with difficult times.

The Importance of a Holistic Approach

Overcoming adversity and coping with difficult times often requires a holistic approach, one that addresses both the physical and emotional aspects of the experience. By combining strategies such as mindfulness, self-compassion, positive thinking, and support from others, individuals can build resilience and find strength in the face of adversity.

Putting it All Together

Start with self-care: Take care of your physical and emotional well-being by engaging in self-care activities, such as exercise, eating a healthy diet, and getting enough sleep.

Practice mindfulness and self-compassion: Mindfulness and self-compassion can help individuals manage stress and anxiety and find inner strength.

Cultivate positive thinking: Focus on the positive aspects of life, and look for opportunities in challenges, to cultivate positive thinking and increase resilience.

Build a support system: Surround yourself with positive, supportive individuals and seek professional support, if necessary, to build a strong support system.

Find purpose and meaning: Engage in meaningful activities, such as volunteering or pursuing hobbies, to find purpose and meaning in difficult times.

Use hope as a tool: Cultivate hope by focusing on positive possibilities and reframing challenges as opportunities for growth and learning.

By combining these strategies, individuals can develop the tools they need to overcome adversity and cope with difficult times.

In conclusion, overcoming adversity is a journey, and each individual's experience will be unique. By embracing a holistic approach, incorporating self-care and positive thinking, building a strong support system, and finding purpose and meaning, individuals can find strength in the face of adversity and emerge even stronger.

"In the face of adversity, resilience and
determination are key to finding success and
happiness."

ೞ

Other Books Of The Author

1. The Moments When I Met God
2. Kashiyile Theertha Pathangal
3. Guru Gyan Vani
4. Abhiprerak Gita
5. Assi Se Jain Ghat Tak
6. Hopelessness Of Arjuna
7. The Soul And It's True Nature
8. Sense Of Action (Karma)
9. Action Through Wisdom
10. Action Through Wisdom
11. Theory And Practical Of Every Action
12. Logical Understanding Of The Supreme
13. The Imperishable Supreme
14. Yatra Nishadraj Se Hanuman Ghat Tak
15. Yatra Karnatak Ghat Se Raja Ghat Tak
16. Yatra Pandey Ghat Se Prayagraj Ghat Tak
17. Yatra Ranjendra Prasad Ghat Se Dattatreya Ghat Tak
18. Yaatrasindhiya Ghat Se Gwaliar Ghat Tak
19. Yatra Mangala Gauri Ghat Se Hanuman Gadhi Ghat Tak
20. Yatra Gaay Ghat Se Nishad Ghat Tak
21. Maa Ganga, Ghaten Evm Utsav
22. Ganga Arti Dev Deepavali Evam Any Utsav
23. Potentials Of Digitalized India
24. Vedic Consciousness
25. A Brief Introduction To Vedic Science
26. Kashi Ke Barah Jyotirling
27. Impact Of Motivation
28. Let's Have A Milky Way Journey
29. Color Therapy In A Nutshell

30. Rigveda In A Nutshell
31. Yajurveda In A Nutshell
32. Samveda In A Nutshell
33. Atharva Veda In A Nutshell
34. Ayushman Bhava - Ayurveda
35. Srimad Bhagavad Gita And Upanishad Connection
36. Srimad Bhagavad Gita - An Attempt To Summarize Each Chapter.
37. Facts And Impact Of Nakshatra
38. Astro Gems - Navaratna
39. Ekadashi - A Concise Overview
40. A Concise View Of Hanuman Chalisa
41. Inspirational Gita
42. Nakshatraranyam
43. Summary Of 18 Mahapuranas
44. Synopsis Of 18 Upa Puranas
45. Rigvediya Upanishads
46. Shukla Yajurvediya Upanishads
47. Krishna Yajurvediya Upanishads
48. Samavediya Upanishads
49. Atharvavediya Upanishads
50. The Seven Great Sages
51. From Rocket Scientist To President Dr. Apj Abdul Kalam
52. The Visionary's Voice - Quotes Of Dr. Apj Abdul Kalam
53. The Wisdom Of Swami Vivekananda: Insights And Inspiration From A Legendary Spiritual Teacher
54. Ayurvedic Remedies From The Garden
55. Sages And Seers
56. Rising Strong – Motivational Stories Of Women
57. Beyond Flames -Mystery Stories Of Funeral Ghat Manikarnika
58. The Origins Of Tulsi: A Look At The Mythological Roots Of The Plant"

59. The Holistic Cow: A Look At The Physical, Spiritual, And Cultural Importance Of Cows In India
60. Arts Of Healing
61. Exploring The Divine
62. Understanding Five Elements
63. The Etymology Of Ram
64. Symbols Of India
65. Voice Of Change (About Speeches Of Great Men)
66. She Speaks (About Speeches Of Great Women)
67. Patriotism On Celluloid – Brief About Patriotic Films
68. The Music Of Motivation: A Brief Guide To Inspirational Film Songs
69. Unlocking The Secrets Of The Dashopanishads
70. A Cultural Mosaic
71. Ancient Traditions, Modern Minds
72. Ecos Of Ancient Wisdom
73. Beneath The Surface
74. From Temples To Ashrams
75. Sages Of The Subcontinent
76. The Art Of Healling (Ayurveda, Yoga & Naturopathy)
77. Indian Kitchen
78. The Festivals Of India
79. The Indian Epics Retold
80. The Power Of Mantras
81. The Indian River Ganges
82. The Indian Architecture
83. Rites Of Passage
84. The Indian Silk Road
85. The Indian Literature
86. The Indian Villages
87. The Indian Folks & Crafts
88. The Way Of Buddha
89. The Ramayan Of Tulsidas

CONTACT

DR. JAGADEESH PILLAI

MBA & PhD in Vedic Science

Four Times Guinness World Record Holder

Winner of Mahatma Gandhi Vishwa Shanti Puraskar and Global Peace Ambassador

Gemology, Astro & Vastu Consultant - Spiritual Counselor

Consultant for designing World Record Ideas

Efficient Tarot Card Reader

9839093003

myrichindia@gmail.com

drjagadeeshpillai@facebook

drjagadeeshpillai@instagram

jagadeeshpillai@youtube

www. JAGADEESHPILLAI.com

|| LOKAHA SAMASTHAHA SUKHINO BHAVANTU ||